Construction

Kay Robertson

© 2014 Rourke Educational Media

All rights reserved. No part of this book may be reproduced or utilized in any form or by any means, electronic or mechanical including photocopying, recording, or by any information storage and retrieval system without permission in writing from the publisher.

www.rourkeeducationalmedia.com

PHOTO CREDITS: Cover: © Andrey Starostin (pyramids), © Scott Prokop (dam), © Cheng HSU-CHU (tunnel), © Nikita Belokhonov (home), © Vitezslav Valka (background), © wajan (Eiffel Tower), © feiyuwzhangjie (Great Wall of China); page 4: ©

Edited by: Luana Mitten

Cover and interior design by: Renee Brady

Library of Congress PCN Data

STEM Guides to Construction / Kay Robertson.
    p. cm. -- (STEM Everyday)
Includes index.
ISBN 978-1-62169-844-9 (hardcover)
ISBN 978-1-62169-739-8 (softcover)
ISBN 978-1-62169-947-7 (e-Book)
Library of Congress Control Number: 2013936449

Rourke Educational Media
Printed in the United States of America,
North Mankato, Minnesota

rourkeeducationalmedia.com
customerservice@rourkeeducationalmedia.com • PO Box 643328 Vero Beach, Florida 32964

Table of Contents

Introduction 4
Pyramids of Egypt 6
The Great Wall 11
Homes 15
Building It Bigger 24
Over Land and Water 33
Conclusion 43
Glossary 44
Index 46
The Metric System 47
Websites to Visit 48
Show What You Know 48

Introduction

Do you like to build things using wooden blocks, Legos, or Lincoln Logs? If you take classes in woodworking or metal, you can construct things like a birdhouse or a spice rack. Maybe you have helped your parents on a bigger construction project like building a doghouse.

You have probably done lots of construction work without even realizing it.

In this book you will take a look at some old construction projects that continue to amaze people because of their vast size. You will examine some of the techniques construction workers use to create the homes we live in today. You will also take a look at the massive skyscraper buildings that can be found in the world's biggest cities. Finally, you will take a look at the bridges and tunnels people have constructed to carry them easily from one spot to another.

Some construction projects are bigger than others, but at the core they are all the same. They are all about measuring, estimating, and calculating. Constructing anything requires a lot of numbers, and wherever there are numbers you can find math!

Pyramids of Egypt

Many of the world's greatest construction projects no longer exist. We only know about them because of ancient writings.

Between the years 484 and 425 BCE there lived a Greek **historian** named Herodotus. Herodotus is sometimes called the "father of history" because he spent much of his life gathering and recording information. Sometime in the 5th Century BCE Herodotus compiled a list of Seven Wonders of the World. This was a list of man-made **structures** so vast and impressive that they were truly wondrous.

Six of the Seven Wonders no longer exist. They were destroyed by natural disasters like floods, fire, and earthquakes.

STEM in Action

How many of the Seven Wonders are still with us today? You can find out by using subtraction:

$$7 - 6 = 1$$

Only 1 of the Seven Wonders is still with us today! That one remaining wonder is the Great Pyramid, located in Giza, Egypt.

STEM Fast Fact

Seven Wonders of the World
1. Great Pyramid of Giza
2. Hanging Gardens of Babylon
3. Statue of Zeus at Olympia
4. Temple of Artemis at Ephesus
5. Mausoleum at Halicarnassus
6. Colossus of Rhodes
7. Lighthouse of Alexandria

The Egyptians made many **pyramids**, but the Great Pyramid is the largest they ever built. The Great Pyramid is roughly 482 feet (146.91 meters) high, and each side measures 756 feet (230.43 meters) at the base.

Khafre's Pyramid is a pyramid in Giza that was constructed sometime after the Great Pyramid was completed. Khafre's Pyramid appears to be larger than the Great Pyramid, but this is only because it is built on higher ground.

The Great Pyramid in Giza, Egypt is the only remaining wonder of the Seven Ancient Wonders of the World.

In fact, the **dimensions** of Khafre's Pyramid are just slightly smaller than those of the Great Pyramid. Khafre's Pyramid has a base measuring 705 feet (214.88 meters) and reaches up to a height of 471 feet (143.56 meters).

Modern man has built bigger and taller structures than the pyramids. The Burj Khalifa in Dubai and the Hoover Dam are just two examples. Both of those structures, though, were built with the aid of powerful machinery. How did the Egyptians build the pyramids without bulldozers, drills, or explosives?

Burj Khalifa reaches up to the height of 2,717 feet (828 meters).

STEM in Action?

How much taller is the Great Pyramid compared to Khafre's Pyramid? Again, finding the answer is simply a matter of subtracting:

$$482 - 471 = 11$$

The Great Pyramid is roughly 11 feet higher than Khafre's Pyramid!

What about the two pyramids' bases? How much larger is the base of the Great Pyramid compared to the base of Khafre's Pyramid?

$$756 - 705 = 51$$

The Great Pyramid has a base 51 feet longer than the base of Khafre's Pyramid!

STEM in Action

About how much does the Great Pyramid weigh? You can find out by using multiplication:

$$5{,}000 \times 2{,}000{,}000 = 10{,}000{,}000{,}000$$

The Great Pyramid weighs about 10 billion pounds!

Experts believe that the Great Pyramid was built over a period of about 20 years. If so, how many stones were put in place each year? You can find out using division:

$$2{,}000{,}000 \div 20 = 100{,}000$$

About 100,000 stones were put in place during each year of the construction of the Great Pyramid!

Using simple tools, the Egyptians first quarried rock from **areas** nearby where a pyramid was to be built. Next, the pyramid base was constructed. Then, using a system of ramps, more rocks were piled on top of the base.

Consider these numbers: The Great Pyramid is **composed** of about 2 million stones, each weighing roughly 5,000 pounds (2,267 kilograms)!

The Hoover Dam is a structure on a scale similar to that of the Great Pyramid, but the Hoover Dam was built using modern equipment.

The Great Pyramid was the world's tallest man-made structure until the Eiffel Tower was built in Paris, France, in 1889.

STEM in Action?

The Eiffel Tower

The Eiffel Tower is 984 feet high. How much taller than the Great Pyramid is the Eiffel Tower?

$$984 - 482 = 502$$

The Eiffel Tower is 502 feet taller than the Great Pyramid!

Look again at the relative heights of the Great Pyramid and the Eiffel Tower:

984   482

Divide the height of the Eiffel Tower by the height of the Great Pyramid:

$$984 \div 482 = 2.04$$

Now you know that 482 multiplied by 2 is about equal to the height of the Eiffel Tower. This means that the Eiffel Tower is roughly twice as tall as the Great Pyramid!

The Great Wall

The Great Wall of China is a massive structure that was built along China's northern border during the 15th and 16th centuries. The original purpose of the Great Wall was to protect China from invasion by Mongolian nomads. Today, however, the Great Wall serves another purpose as a tourist attraction.

The Great Wall of China isn't especially tall. It only has an **average** height of 25 feet (762 centimeters). What is truly remarkable about the Great Wall is its length. Although it is not a single **continuous** structure, the Great Wall covers at least a distance of about 1,500 miles (2,414 kilometers), and some **estimates** are even longer than that!

If the Great Wall of China covers about half the distance across North America, how many Great Walls would it take to cover the entire distance?

STEM in Action?

If there are 5,280 feet in one mile, how many feet long is the Great Wall of China? You can find out by using multiplication:

$$5{,}280 \times 1{,}500 = 7{,}920{,}000$$

The Great Wall of China is about 8 million feet long!

Let's look at that another way. From the east coast to the west coast, the continent of North America is about 3,000 miles across. How can we compare those distances?

$$1{,}500 \qquad 3{,}000$$

Try dividing the distance covered by the Great Wall of China by the distance from one coast of North America to the other:

$$1{,}500 \div 3{,}000 = 0.5$$

So the Great Wall of China is roughly half as long as the distance from one coast of North America to the other! That's a big wall!

Can you figure out about how much of the wall each worker was responsible for building? For this calculation, you're going to use the length of the wall measured in feet and the number of workers:

$$7{,}920{,}000 \div 300{,}000 = 26.4$$

Each laborer on the Great Wall built about 26 feet!

One thing to remember is that the Great Wall was constructed over a period of thousands of years. And, while guesses can be made, we may never be sure precisely how many people helped build the Great Wall. One estimate places the number of workers at around 300,000.

The achievement of the Great Wall of China is made more impressive when you realize that it was built by hand!

The idea that the Great Wall can be seen from outer space is only a myth.

STEM Fast Fact

Visible From the Moon?

One myth surrounding the Great Wall of China is that it is the only man-made structure big enough to be seen from outer space, and possibly even from the Moon. This is incorrect. In low Earth orbit, which is about 160 miles (257.50 kilometers) to 350 miles (563.27 kilometers) above the Earth, astronauts can see a number of man-made objects. However, the Great Wall is barely visible. Needless to say, if the Great Wall isn't visible from this distance, it certainly isn't visible from the Moon, which is approximately 237,500 miles (381,414.53 meters) away from Earth!

Homes

It is not unusual for families to live in apartment buildings or condominiums, especially in big cities. Other families live in houses, or structures intended for a small number of people.

Not all houses look alike, but they are all constructed according to the same guidelines. These building **codes** ensure that the homes being made are structurally sound.

The men and women who build houses follow plans called blueprints. These plans make sure the homes they create are sturdy and safe.

Think about this for a second. How would you construct a house? Would you build the roof first? Of course not! A roof needs something to rest on before it can be built! That is why houses are always built from the ground up. In a way, it's just like making a house of cards. You use a table or some other flat surface as the base, then prop up cards vertically for the walls, and then lay other cards down horizontally for the roof.

Let's start with the first thing a house needs. It needs a solid base that it can sit on. This is called a foundation.

Basically, there are three types of foundations: basements, crawl spaces, and **slabs**. A basement is a large hole dug into the earth, usually at a depth of about 8 feet (243.84 centimeters). A crawl space means that the house rests on a series of cinder blocks that raise the house above the earth. A slab, meanwhile, is a flat surface of concrete much like a parking lot or an outdoor basketball court.

When the foundation of a house is completed, a floor can be constructed. Floors are typically built with pieces of 2x10 wood, or lumber. That description probably looks to you like a multiplication problem. In this case, though, the "x" should be read as "by." So the piece of lumber would be a "two by ten."

STEM in Action

Consider some other common lumber sizes:

1x2

2x4

4x4

Let's compare a 1x2 and a 2x4. How much thicker is a 2x4 compared to a 1x2? You can find out by using subtraction. Just subtract the smaller number from the larger number:

$$2 - 1 = 1$$

A 2x4 is exactly 1 inch thicker than a 1x2!

What about width? How much wider is a 2x4 compared to a 1x2?

$$4 - 2 = 2$$

A 2x4 is 2 inches wider than a 1x2!

Now compare a 4x4 and a 1x2. How much bigger is a 4x4 than a 1x2? First, calculate for the thickness:

$$4 - 1 = 3$$

Next, calculate for the width:

$$4 - 2 = 2$$

A 4x4 is 3 inches thicker and 2 inches wider than a 1x2!

Lumber, or wood, comes in all sorts of shapes and sizes. What size you'll need depends on the job you're doing.

There are different ways of sizing pieces of lumber. The most common, though, is to measure the thickness and the width. When a piece of lumber is described as a 2x10, what is really being said is that the piece of lumber is 2 inches (5.08 centimeters) thick by 10 inches (25.4 centimeters) wide.

Building A Floor

To create the floor, you are going to lay down 2x10s at an equal spacing of 19 inches (48.26 centimeters). Without considering the frame that will connect all the 2x10s together, how many 2x10s will you need to make a floor that is 30 feet (9.14 meters) long?

STEM in Action

First of all, you need to know how long 30 feet is in terms of inches. There are 12 inches in a foot, so how many inches are there in 30 feet? You can find out by multiplying:

$$12 \times 30 = 360$$

There are 360 inches in 30 feet! Next, you need to divide 360 inches by the spacing of your 2x10s—19 inches:

$$360 \div 19 = 18.9$$

To create a floor 30 feet long you will need about 19 2x10s!

The walls of a house are not constructed vertically. Rather, they are assembled on the house's foundation and then raised into place.

Building the Walls

The next step in building a house is the construction of the walls. Walls are made with 2x4s. To ensure maximum support for the roof, a 2x4 is placed every 16 inches (40.64 centimeters).

If the walls for your imaginary home are each 30 feet (9.14 meters) long, how many 2x4s will you need for 4 walls?

STEM in Action

From the last problem, you already know there are 360 inches in 30 feet, so:

$$360 \div 16 = 22.5$$

To create a wall 30 feet long you will need about 23 2x4s! How many 2x4s are you going to need for 4 walls?

$$4 \times 23 = 92$$

To create 4 walls you will need 92 2x4s!

Raising the Roof

With the walls of the house built and secured in place, you can move on to the roof.

A roof can be made from scratch, but it is very common nowadays for roofs to be constructed using **pre-made** triangular structures called **trusses**. These are lowered onto the top of the house frame using cranes and can be put up very quickly.

Just like your floor and walls, the trusses that form your roof will be positioned at equal spacings.

In real life, there would be several more details to attend to before your house could be considered finished. These would include installing insulation, electrical wiring, and siding. In the case of your imaginary home, though, you are done!

STEM in Action

In the case of the roof trusses, this distance will be 24 inches. How many trusses will you need for a roof 30 feet long?

$$360 \div 24 = 15$$

You'll need 15 trusses!

Calculating area is especially easy if you have blueprints that note the exact measurements for the house.

STEM in Action

Area

Area is a measure of size for a flat surface. Take your bedroom, for instance. How big is it? Different shapes require different formulas for calculating area, but as long as your bedroom is rectangular, finding the area is actually very simple. First, you need to measure the lengths of two connecting walls. Let's say that the lengths of your two walls are 10 feet and 14 feet. To find the area of your room, all you need to do is multiply those two numbers:

10 x 14 = 140

The area of your room is 140 square feet!

Calculating the area of your imaginary house can be done in exactly the same way. You know that each side is 30 feet long, so:

30 x 30 = 900

Your imaginary home measures 900 square feet!

Building It Bigger

The ability to make safe, solid, comfortable houses is quite an achievement. Still, when you think about really impressive construction projects, nothing seems quite as remarkable as the skyscraper. In many ways, skyscrapers are the modern-day versions of massive building projects like the Pyramids and the Great Wall.

A large structure like a pyramid had to have a massive base to support its enormous weight. The brilliance of the skyscraper is that, instead of using an expanded base, it uses a kind of **skeleton** made of iron and steel **girders** to support its weight. Each girder rests on a large concrete foot that keeps it upright. Inventions like the elevator, meanwhile, made very tall buildings a practical possibility.

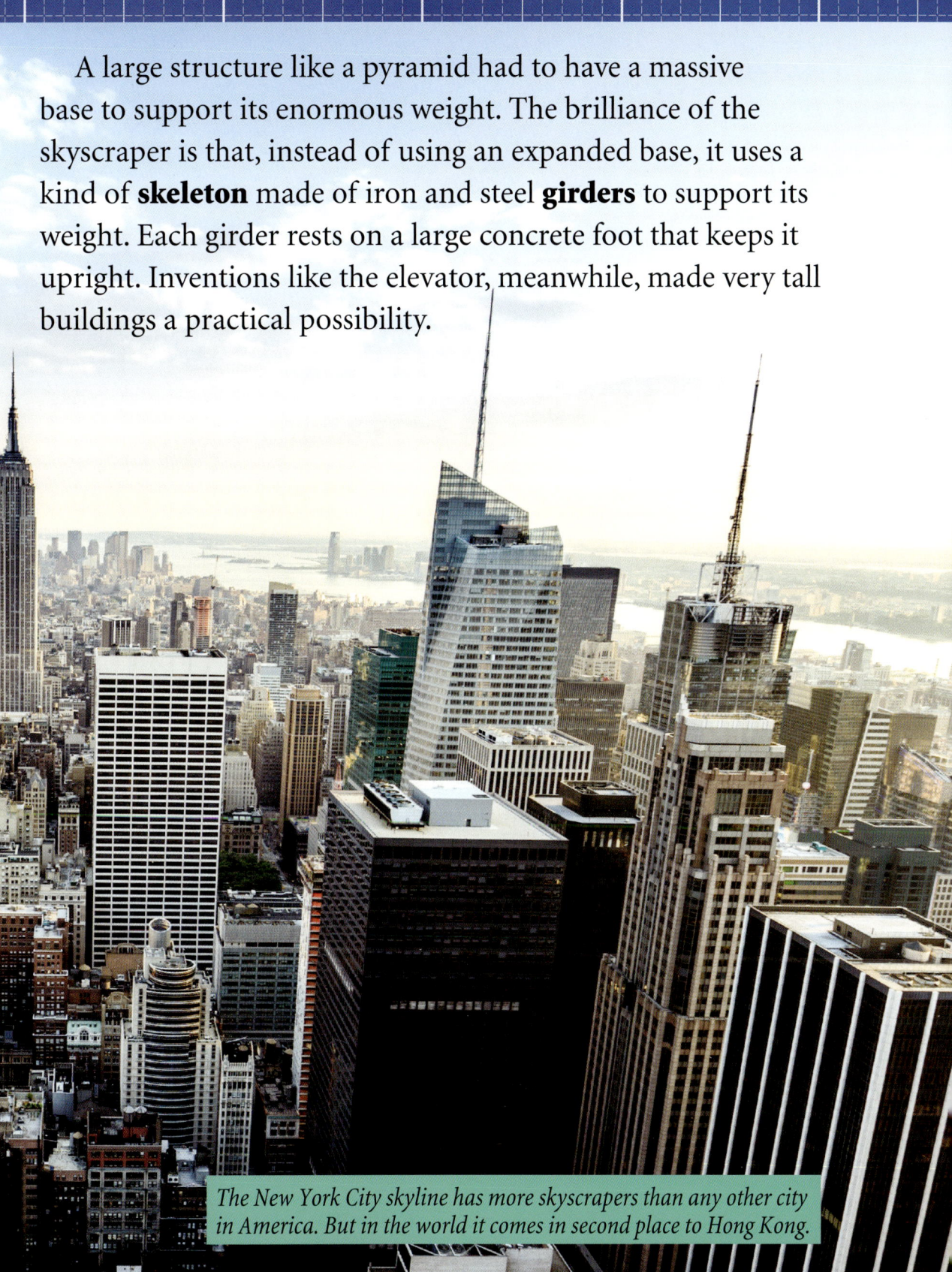

The New York City skyline has more skyscrapers than any other city in America. But in the world it comes in second place to Hong Kong.

STEM in Action

Using the map below can you find the answers to the following questions:

What is the name of the tallest building in the world?

What is the name of the 10th tallest building in the world?

What is the difference between the number of stories in the building with the most stories and the building with the least stories?

Willis Tower

Chicago, USA
108 Stories
1,451 feet (442 meters)

One World Trade Center

New York City, USA
104 Stories
1,776 feet (541 meters)

STEM in Action

Can you figure out how many feet taller the Taipei 101 building is compared to the International Commerce Centre?

1670 − 1588 = 82

The Taipei 101 building is 82 feet taller than the International Commerce Centre!

Taipei 101, Taipei

International Commerce Center, Hong Kong

STEM in Action

An average is a number that represents a group of numbers. For instance, imagine yourself and two friends. Let's say that you measure how tall you are. Here are the measurements:

4.5 feet
5 feet
5.2 feet

How would you calculate your average height? First, add the heights together:

$$4.5 + 5 + 5.2 = 14.7$$

The next step is to divide that number by the number of **addends**. Addends are simply the numbers you added together. In this case, there were three addends, so:

$$14.7 \div 3 = 4.9$$

The average height for you and your two friends is 4.9 feet tall!

Elevators are one of the things that make skyscrapers practical. Today the elevators in some skyscrapers can travel nearly 38 miles per hour (61 kilometers per hour).

Even though there are more numbers involved, calculating the average height of the world's ten tallest buildings works exactly the same way.

STEM in Action?

First, add the individual heights together:

$$2{,}717 + 1{,}972 + 1{,}776 + 1{,}671 + 1{,}614 + 1{,}588 + 1{,}483 + 1{,}483 + 1{,}476 + 1{,}451 = 17{,}231$$

The combined height of the ten buildings is 17,231 feet!

The second step is to divide that result by the number of addends, 10:

$$17{,}231 \div 10 = 1{,}723.1$$

The average height of the ten tallest buildings is roughly 1,723 feet!

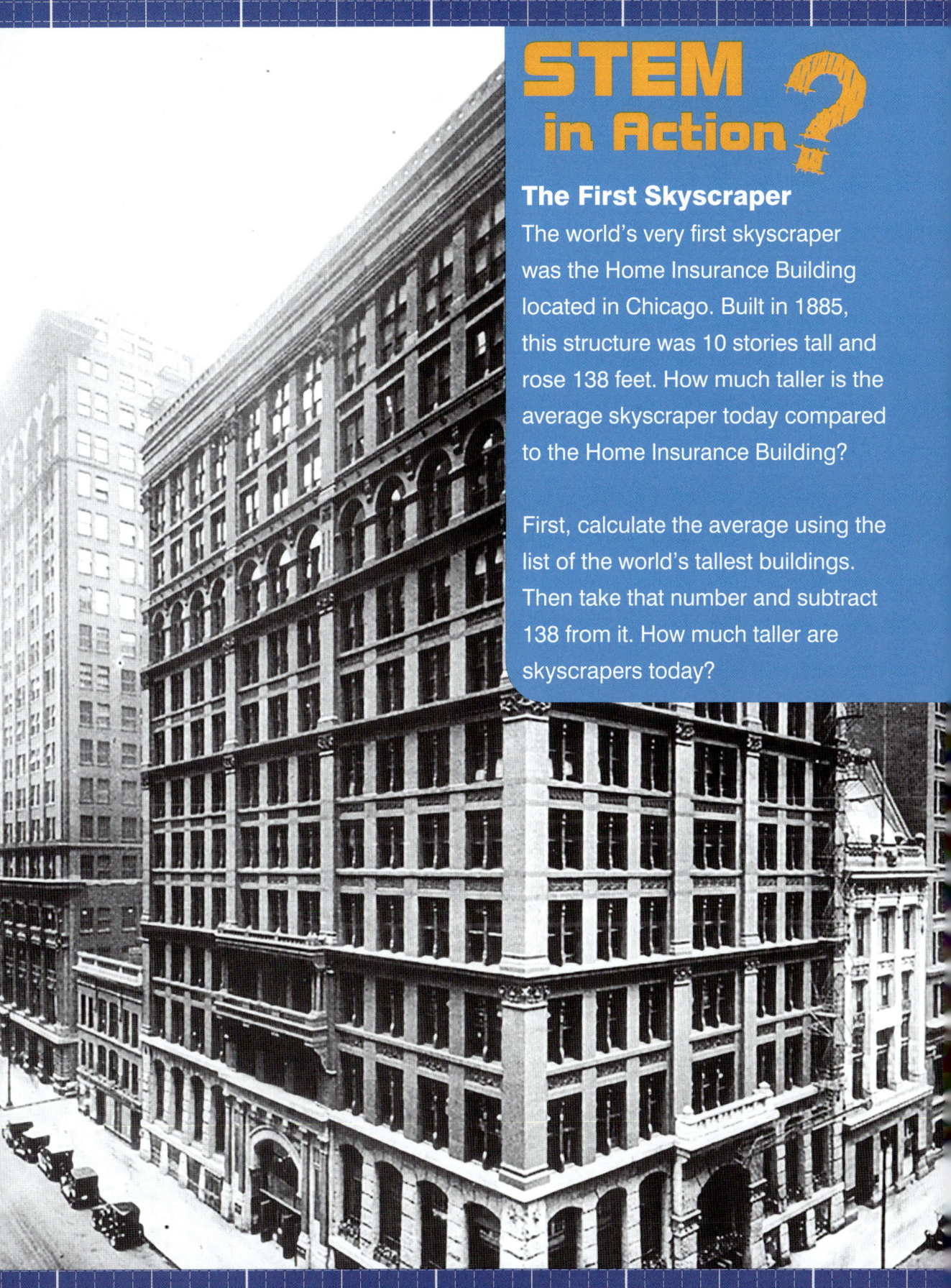

STEM in Action

The First Skyscraper

The world's very first skyscraper was the Home Insurance Building located in Chicago. Built in 1885, this structure was 10 stories tall and rose 138 feet. How much taller is the average skyscraper today compared to the Home Insurance Building?

First, calculate the average using the list of the world's tallest buildings. Then take that number and subtract 138 from it. How much taller are skyscrapers today?

The distance between supports on a bridge is called a span.

Over Land and Water

There are other kinds of structures that are not meant for people to stay in, but are just as important. One of these structures is the bridge.

Simply put, a bridge is a tool that allows people to cross over something like a body of water or the distance between two peaks over a valley. Do you have stepping stones leading from your driveway to the front door of your house? Even those are a kind of bridge that let you get from one place to the other while avoiding something in between, like the grass.

Let's consider three types of bridges:

Beam Bridges
Arch Bridges
Suspension Bridges

There are a number of ways in which these structures differ. The most important thing, though, is the difference in **span**. Remember earlier when you were building your house how the pieces of wood used to create the floor, walls, and roof were evenly spaced for support? Bridges use a similar design pattern. The distance between two bridge supports is called a span.

STEM in Action?

Here are the spans for the three types of bridges:

Beam Bridges = 200 feet
Arch Bridges = 800 feet
Suspension Bridges = 7,000 feet

How much greater is the span of an arch bridge compared to the span of a beam bridge? You can find out by subtracting the smaller number from the larger number:

800 − 200 = 600

The span of an arch bridge is roughly 600 feet greater than the span of a beam bridge!

How much greater is the span of a suspension bridge compared to the span of an arch bridge?

7,000 − 800 = 6,200

The span of a suspension bridge is roughly 6,200 feet greater than the span of an arch bridge!

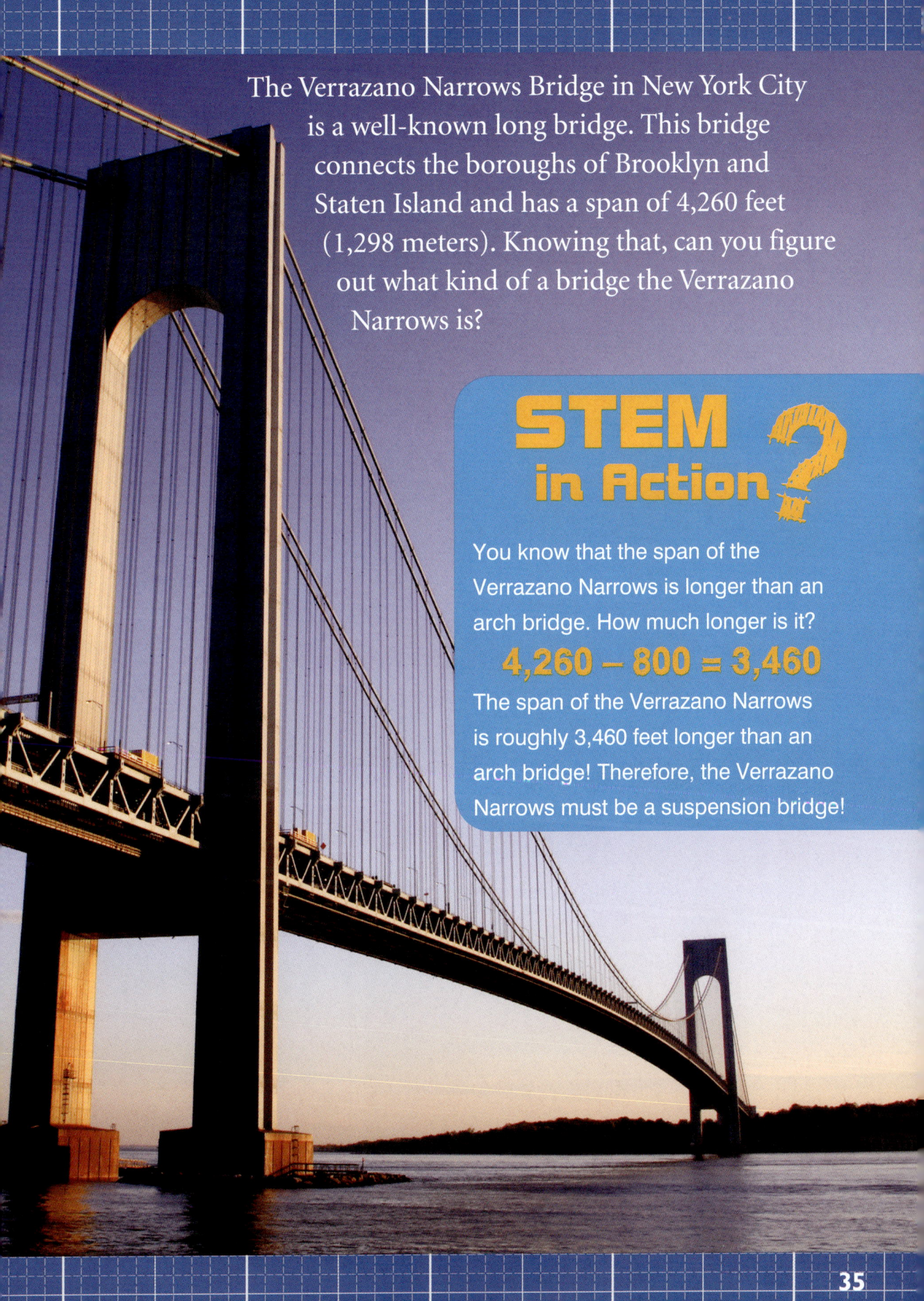

The Verrazano Narrows Bridge in New York City is a well-known long bridge. This bridge connects the boroughs of Brooklyn and Staten Island and has a span of 4,260 feet (1,298 meters). Knowing that, can you figure out what kind of a bridge the Verrazano Narrows is?

STEM in Action

You know that the span of the Verrazano Narrows is longer than an arch bridge. How much longer is it?

$$4{,}260 - 800 = 3{,}460$$

The span of the Verrazano Narrows is roughly 3,460 feet longer than an arch bridge! Therefore, the Verrazano Narrows must be a suspension bridge!

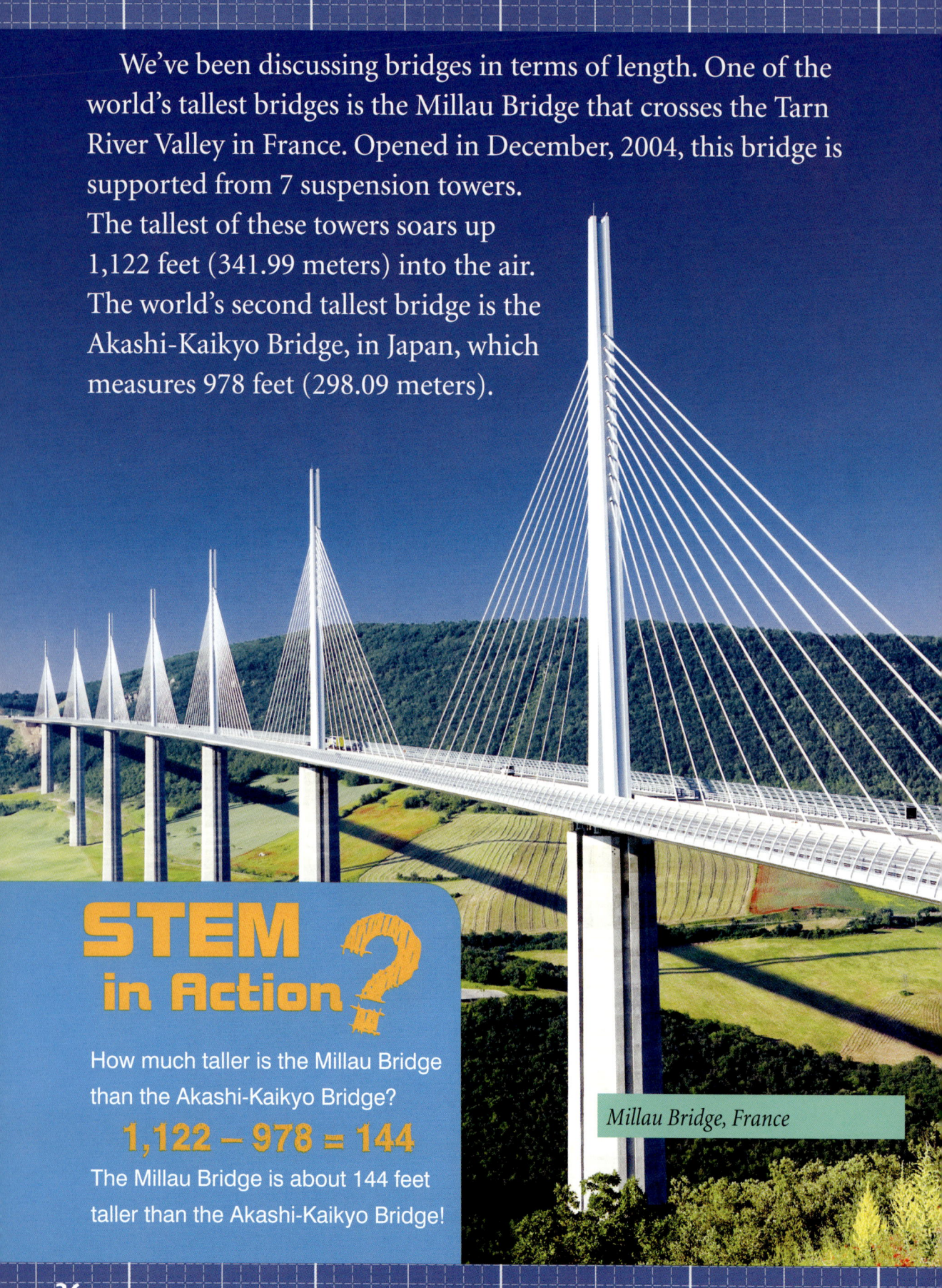

We've been discussing bridges in terms of length. One of the world's tallest bridges is the Millau Bridge that crosses the Tarn River Valley in France. Opened in December, 2004, this bridge is supported from 7 suspension towers. The tallest of these towers soars up 1,122 feet (341.99 meters) into the air. The world's second tallest bridge is the Akashi-Kaikyo Bridge, in Japan, which measures 978 feet (298.09 meters).

STEM in Action

How much taller is the Millau Bridge than the Akashi-Kaikyo Bridge?

1,122 − 978 = 144

The Millau Bridge is about 144 feet taller than the Akashi-Kaikyo Bridge!

Millau Bridge, France

Bridges allow you to cross bodies of water and valleys because they are built over them. But there is another kind of structure that addresses the same problem by traveling under the ground. This structure is the tunnel.

There are many different kinds of tunnels. The kind of tunnel is usually defined by what is traveling through it. Railway tunnels, for instance, are meant for trains. Vehicular tunnels are meant for vehicles like cars and trucks.

STEM in Action

The world's longest railway tunnel is the Seikan Tunnel in Japan. The Seikan Tunnel is located 800 feet under the sea. It runs a total distance of 33.5 miles. How many feet is that?

33.5 x 5,280 = 176,880

The Seikan Tunnel is about 177,000 feet long!

The second-longest tunnel in the world is the Channel Tunnel, also called the Chunnel. This structure connects Great Britain and France over a distance of 31.3 miles. How much longer is the Seikan Tunnel compared to the Chunnel?

33.5 − 31.3 = 2.2

The Seikan Tunnel is roughly 2.2 miles longer than the Chunnel!

Both the Seikan Tunnel and the Chunnel are railway tunnels. The world's longest vehicular tunnel is the St. Gotthard Tunnel located in the Swiss Alps. The St. Gotthard tunnel is 10.2 miles long. How does it compare to the world's longest railway tunnel, the Seikan?

33.5 − 10.2 = 23.3

The St. Gotthard Tunnel is approximately 23 miles shorter than the Seikan Tunnel!

Channel Tunnel

One of the most famous arches in the world is the Gateway Arch in St. Louis, Missouri. This structure stands 630 feet (192.02 meters) tall.

STEM Fast Fact

The Arch

An arch is a structure in the shape of a curve or bow, kind of like the letter "u" turned upside down.

It might not look like it, but the arch is one of the strongest structures ever developed. This is because the arch's unique design shifts any pressure on the top to the two outer supporting legs. Arches are so strong that many built by the Romans a thousand years ago are still standing today.

Conclusion

As you have seen, construction projects are very complicated. Many different people have to be involved in order for something to be built.

If this sounds like a world you would like to be a part of, there are many ways you can join in. If you would like to design buildings, homes, and bridges, you can study to become an engineer or an architect. If you would like to actually work with the lumber, steel, and concrete used to make buildings and homes, you can go into construction.

In all these cases, you will be using math to do your job!

GLOSSARY

addends (AD-ends): the numbers added together in an addition problem

arch bridges (ahrch brij-iz): bridges supported by an arch

area (AIR-ee-uh): the measure of a flat surface

average (AV-ur-ij): a number used to represent a group of numbers

beam bridges (beem brij-iz): bridges supported by two beams, one at each end

composed (kuhm-POHZD): what an object is made of

continuous (kuhn-TIN-yoo-uhs): goes on and on without stopping

dimensions (duh-MEN-shuhnz): the way we measure objects with length, width, or height

estimates (ES-tuh-mitz): a guess or rough calculation about an amount, distance, or quantity

girders (GUR-durz): beams made of steel

metric (MET-rik): the system of measurement used by most of the world; the International System of Units

modern (MAH-durn): current, using the latest technology

pre-made (pri-MADE): made in advance

pyramids (PIR-uh-midz): three-dimensional figures with a square base and four triangular sides

skeleton (SKEL-uh-tuhn): the system of bones inside the human body; girders that support a skyscraper

slabs (slabs): flat surfaces that some homes rest on; something like a driveway

span (span): the distance between two supports on a bridge

suspension bridges (suh-SPEN-chuhn brij-iz): bridges supported by a series of cables overhead

trusses (truhs-iz): triangular structures that form the roof of a house

INDEX

arch   33, 34, 35, 40
arch bridges   33, 34
area(s)   9, 23
basement(s)   17
beam bridges   33, 34
bridges   5, 33, 36, 37
calculating   5, 23, 30
condominiums   15
construction workers   5
crawl spaces   17
Egyptians   7, 8, 9
Eiffel Tower   10
elevator   25, 30
engineer   43
estimating   5
foundation(s)   17, 20
girders   25
Giza, Egypt   6, 7
Great Pyramid   6, 7, 8, 9, 10

Great Wall of China   11, 12, 13, 14
Hoover Dam   8, 9
houses   15, 16, 24
Khafre's Pyramid   7, 8
lumber   17, 18, 43
metric system   47
railway tunnels   37, 38
roof   16, 21, 22, 34
skeleton   25
skyscrapers   24, 25, 30, 31
slabs   17
span   32, 34, 35
suspension bridges   33, 34
trusses   22
tunnels   5, 37, 38
vehicular tunnels   37
Verrazano Narrows Bridge   35
walls   16, 20, 21, 24, 34

The Metric System

We actually have two systems of weights and measures in the United States. Quarts, pints, gallons, ounces, and pounds are all units of the U.S. Customary System, also known as the Imperial System.

The other system of measurement, and the only one sanctioned by the United States Government, is the **metric** system, which is also known as the International System of Units. French scientists developed the metric system in the 1790s. The basic unit of measurement in the metric system is the meter, which is about one ten-millionth the distance from the North Pole to the equator.

A metal bar used to represent the length of the standard meter was even created. This bar was replaced in the 1980s, though, when scientists changed the standard of measurement for the meter to a portion of the distance traveled by light in a vacuum.

Converting Imperial to Metric			
Convert	To	Multiply by	Example
inches (in)	millimeters (mm)	25.40	2in x 25.40 = 50.8mm
inches (in)	centimeters (cm)	2.54	2in x 2.54 = 5.08cm
feet (ft)	meters (m)	0.30	2ft x .30 = 0.6m
yards (yd)	meters (m)	0.91	2yd x .91 = 1.82m
miles (mi)	kilometers (km)	1.61	2mi x 1.61 = 3.22km
miles per hour (mph)	kilometers per hour (km/h)	1.61	2mph x 1.61 = 3.22km/h
ounces (oz)	grams (g)	28.35	2oz x 28.35 = 56.7g
pounds (lb)	kilograms (kg)	0.454	2lb x .454 = 0.908kg
tons (T)	metric ton (MT)	1.016	2T x 1.016 = 2.032
ounces (oz)	milliliters (ml)	29.57	2oz x 29.57 = 59.14ml
pint (pt)	liter (l)	0.55	2pt x .55 = 1.1l
quarts (qt)	liters (l)	0.95	2qt x .95 = 1.9l
gallons (gal)	liters (l)	3.785	2gal x 3.785 = 7.57

Websites to Visit

www.pbs.org/wgbh/nova/egypt/explore/khafre.html
NOVA Online – Mysteries of the Nile, the Khafre Pyramid

home.howstuffworks.com/house.htm
How Stuff Works – How House Construction Works

science.howstuffworks.com/bridge.htm
How Stuff Works – How Bridges Work

Show What You Know

1. How did the Egyptians build pyramids without bulldozers, drills, or explosives?

2. How has the Great Wall of China changed?

3. What are three types of bridges and how do they differ from one another?